A New True Book

MUSEUMS

By Janet Papajani

This "true book" was prepared
under the direction of
Illa Podendorf,
formerly with the Laboratory School,
University of Chicago

CHILDRENS PRESS, CHICAGO

For my Grandmother

Christopher Columbus exhibit

PHOTO CREDITS

James P. Rowan—2, 4 (bottom), 11, 17, 21 (4 photos), 22 (2 photos), 24 (2 photos), 27, 28, 31, 32, 42 (right)

Reinhard Brucker—29

Smithsonian Institution: National Museum of Natural History—4 (top), 26
  National Air and Space Museum—41 (2 photos)

German Information Center—10 (left)

Hillstrom Stock Photos—©1982 Laurel Spingola—6
  ©Ray Hillstrom—13 (top right), 15, 16, 18 (left), 35 (2 photos), 42 (left), 45

Tony Freeman—Cover, 33, 37

Chandler Forman—8, 9, 10 (right), 13 (top left, bottom right), 18 (right)

Bill Thomas—13 (bottom left), 14

New York Department of Commerce—39 (2 photos)

Library of Congress Cataloging in Publication Data
Papajani, Janet.
  Museums.
  (A New true book)
  Includes index.
  Summary: A simple introduction to various types of
museums describing their purpose, collections, and
methods of display.
  1. Museums—Juvenile literature. [1. Museums]
I. Title.
AM5.P19 1983   069.5   82-23621
ISBN 0-516-01682-2   AACR2

TABLE OF CONTENTS

Above: Skeleton of
a woolly elephant
Right: Woman shows
how hand-dipped
candles were made.

WHAT IS A MUSEUM?

A museum is a special place. It is a place for seeing and learning about all kinds of things.

Have you ever wondered how tall a giant elephant might be? Or how the inside of your heart looks? Have you ever seen a painting by a famous artist? Or watched someone make candles?

Metropolitan Museum of Art in New York City

By visiting museums you can see and learn about all these things and much more.

HOW MUSEUMS BEGAN

People have always collected and kept things they thought were unusual, beautiful, or important.

Alexander the Great, the famous Greek general, collected samples of rocks, plants, animals, and art objects from all the lands he conquered. He wanted to share what he found with his people. Because

Greek vase on display
at the Athens Museum
in Athens, Greece

of Alexander, the ancient Greeks were the first people to have museums. Today museums also collect and keep samples of special objects to help us all understand and learn about our past and the world around us.

ART MUSEUMS

At an art museum you can see paintings, drawings, statues, sculptures, and other art objects.

The Guggenheim Museum in New York City features modern art.

Above: This modern painting, *Head of a Woman*, hangs at the Guggenheim Museum.
Right: Dürer painted this portrait of his father in 1497. It is shown at the National Gallery in London.

Art museums try to show the "best" samples of an artist's work. Some of the art may be hundreds of years old; others may be just a few years old. All the art is there for you to study and enjoy.

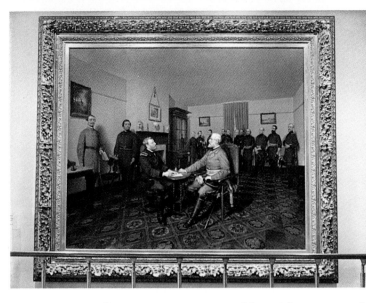

This painting shows an historical event—General Lee surrendering to General Grant at Appomattox Court House. This surrender marked the end of the War Between the States.

As you walk through an art museum you may see paintings or drawings about people, the outdoors, or events in history. Pick out a painting you really like and study it. Try to see what the artist saw or felt about the subject in the painting.

Art museums also have statues and sculptures in their collections. Sculptures are three-dimensional objects. They have height, they have width, and they have depth. You can see all around them. You are a three-dimensional object.

Art can be real and lifelike or it may look like nothing you have ever seen before.

Above left: Sculpture of Nefertiti of Egypt,
              Dahlena Museum in West Berlin, Germany
Above right: Example of modern sculpture
Below right: A Roman sculpture
              in a museum in Paris, France
Below Left: Sculpture on exhibit
              at the Cowboy Museum in Wyoming

At an art museum, the
labels tell you the name of
the artist, the name of the
painting, and when it was
painted. Visiting an art
museum can help you look
at something in a new way.

HISTORY MUSEUMS

History museums usually collect things that show how life may have been in another time or at another place.

Room in the Belmont Mansion Museum in Newport, Rhode Island

A history museum may
have rooms of furniture
that show how people
lived years ago. Or there
may be a store from a
hundred years ago.

At another part of the museum you might see what life was like for the American Indians on the plains. You might even see a collection of toys that once were popular.

Exhibit showing Plains Indians hunting bison

Above: Old bottle-capping machine at
the LaCrosse Historical Society
in Wisconsin.
Right: Old, wooden, hand-operated
printing press at the Gutenberg
Museum in West Germany

History museums save
rare and expensive objects.
They also save everyday
things such as dishes,
newspapers, clothing, and
pictures. All these things

show how people lived at different times in history.

Someday, a Pac-Man game, Smurf dolls, and skateboards may be shown in a history museum. They will help someone in 2020 understand what life was like in the 1980s.

A history museum can also be an outdoor village. Some outdoor history museums look like towns in the Wild West.

Williamsburg in Virginia is an outdoor history museum. This village shows the crafts and folk art of the 1700s. Local people dress and act like the "natives" of a colonial town. They make candles, bind books, make silver objects, make wigs, and build furniture.

Watching these people can make you feel as if you were back in time.

At Williamsburg visitors can see the militia fire their
cannon (above left), watch a glassblower at work (above right), ride
in a horse-drawn carriage (below left), and see how people
dressed in the 1700s (below right).

Henry Winkler as Fonzy,
a character on "Happy
Days," a TV show

Robert Redford as the Sundance Kid (left) and
Paul Newman as Butch Cassidy as
they appeared in a popular movie.

A wax museum is
another type of museum.
Wax figures of famous
people are on display.
Sometimes a tape
recording is played in the
background. It makes the
wax figure seem to be
alive and talking.

Homes of presidents can also be history museums. George Washington's home in Mount Vernon, Virginia; Thomas Jefferson's home in Monticello, Virginia; and Franklin D. Roosevelt's home in Hyde Park, New York, are all history museums. Each house has the furniture, books, and everyday objects used by the president who lived there. They are on display for everyone to see.

Left: Thomas Jefferson's home, Monticello
Right: Figures showing Abraham Lincoln and some of his aides in 1861

Look carefully at the exhibits in a history museum. See what the people wore, what their homes were like, and what they enjoyed doing. Then you will be able to understand what life was like for those people.

NATURAL HISTORY MUSEUMS

Natural history museums show stuffed animals, insects, fish, birds, plants, rocks, and other objects of nature.

Natural history museums try to show the history of the earth, how it has changed over the years, and how it has stayed the same.

Natural history museums also show how people lived long ago. You can see scenes about cave people. The cave people may be hunting for small animals or cooking their food. You can see that life was hard for the cave people.

Reconstruction of a Neanderthal burial ceremony held 20,000 years ago

Scene showing early mound builders

Other exhibits may show
the life of the American
Indians. You may see a
scene of how a family
worked together to plant
corn, how the women
ground the corn into flour,
and cooked the family

Apache wickiup

meal over a fire. The Indians dressed in leather clothing made from animal skins. Indians, like most early people, depended on nature for their clothing and shelter.

Dinosaur skeleton on display in the main hall of the
Field Museum in Chicago

One of the most popular
exhibits at a natural history
museum is the dinosaur
display. Since dinosaurs
were such large animals,

their skeletons usually stand about ten feet tall. Looking at a skeleton you can imagine how frightening it would be if dinosaurs were alive today.

Natural history museums may also have displays of insects from all over the world. Some are very beautiful and have brightly colored wings and markings.

This man is a taxidermist. A taxidermist prepares, stuffs, and mounts the skins of animals shown in museums.

The people who work at natural history museums are always studying and learning. They collect many samples of rocks, plants, insects, and animals. They want to make their exhibits interesting and as complete as possible.

Display showing life in the sea nearly four million years ago

Natural history museums help us learn about the animals, insects, fish, and plants of the world. When you visit a natural history museum try to see how all of nature fits together.

SCIENCE MUSEUMS

Science museums are very popular. These museums usually have exhibits that move. You can push buttons, pull levers, and use computers.

Display showing how gears and cams operate

The exhibits in a science museum help explain how things work.

There may be exhibits about the human body. Some exhibits might explain how the body uses food for building muscles and growing bones. There might be a giant model of the human heart. You can walk through it and see the inside of it. You can even hear it beating.

Other displays can show how science is used to

make things better. There might be exhibits on electricity, computers, telephones, and television. You can learn how something first began, how it works, and how it may be used in the future.

Left: Perpetual motion exhibit. Right: Example of a 1930s' telephone

There may also be a farm exhibit. You can see how a farmer plants and harvests crops with tractors, combines, and other farm equipment. You may even see how an incubator helps a baby chick hatch from its shell. Or how milking machines are used to milk cows.

Science museums are always changing. The people who work there try to make the exhibits easy

Visitors watch a coil make lightning.

to understand, exciting to
watch, and interesting to
operate. When you visit a
museum enjoy yourself and
try to learn something
about how science helps
us live better lives.

SPECIAL INTEREST MUSEUMS

Some museums collect objects about only one subject. These museums are called special interest museums.

The baseball museum in Cooperstown, New York is a special interest museum. It is all about baseball. The exhibits tell the history of baseball and show the

At the Baseball Hall of Fame in Cooperstown, New York, visitors can look at displays of the items used by famous players and different teams. They may also have a chance to see how an automatic pitching machine operates (right).

uniforms and equipment of famous baseball players. Anyone interested in baseball would want to visit this museum.

The Air and Space Museum in Washington, D.C. is another special interest museum. It tells the complete story of air travel and space flights. The first airplane flown by the Wright brothers is on display. It also tells the story of the space missions. The equipment and space suits used by the astronauts to land on the moon are also shown.

The Wright 1903 Flyer (above) was the first, powered, heavier-than-air craft to achieve controlled flight. The Lunar Roving Vehicle carried astronauts around on the moon.

Above: View of child's bedroom in the Villa Louis Mansion. This was the home of the first governor of the Territory of Wisconsin. Right: Old-time steam engine operated at the LaPorte County Steam Museum in Indiana.

Special interest museums can be about any subject. There are museums that tell the story of cartooning and comic strips, circuses, and antique cars. Some small museums may be about dolls, glass, trolley cars, or clocks.

The U.S.S. *Intrepid,* an aircraft carrier, has been turned into a Sea and Air Museum. It is anchored in New York City on the Hudson River. It has airplanes from 1911 to planes used in World War II. The exhibits are there for people to see and touch.

VISITING A MUSEUM

When you do visit a museum try to take your time looking at the exhibits and objects on display.

Read the labels next to the objects.

There may even be pamphlets about special exhibits that tell you about the history of the exhibits.

You can find museums all over the world. There are museums in cities, in small towns, and in the country. No matter where a museum might be it is there for people to visit, to learn, and to have fun.

Cars from the Antique Auto Museum in Kansas City.

WORDS YOU SHOULD KNOW

colonial(Kuh • LOAN • ee • il) — having to do with the time when America was a young country

combine(KOM • byne) — a farm machine that cuts and cleans grain

conquer(KAHNG • ker) — to get control over

dimension(dih • MEN • shun) — the measure of how far something is in length, width, and height

Neanderthal(nee • ANN • der • thawl) — relating to Stone Age humans that once lived in Europe, northern Africa, and western Asia

outlaw(OUT • law) — a person who breaks the law; a criminal

plains(PLAYNZ) — large, flat areas of land without any trees

rare(RAIR) — not found or seen too often

sculpture(SKULP • cher) — a piece of art made by shaping clay, carving wood or stone, or pouring liquid metal into a mold

taxidermist(TAX • ih • derm • ist) — person who is trained to prepare, stuff, and mount skins of animals.

wickiup(WICK • ee • up) — hut used by wandering Indian tribes in western and southwestern parts of the United States

INDEX

About the Author

Janet Papajani received her undergraduate degree from Western Michigan University and her master's degree from Syracuse University. She has been a speech therapist, an editor, and a producer of audio-visual materials for student and professional audiences. The author is now associated with Motivation Media, a marketing communication company located in the Midwest.

The True Book of Museums *is the first book she has published for Childrens Press. Janet likes to visit museums of all kinds. . . "Museums are fun. They are a wonderful way to learn about many different subjects."*